Mutiny at Crossbones Bay

Written, designed and illustrated by Mark Burgess

Edited by Phil Roxbee Cox

Assistant editor: Michelle Bates

Series editor: Gaby Waters

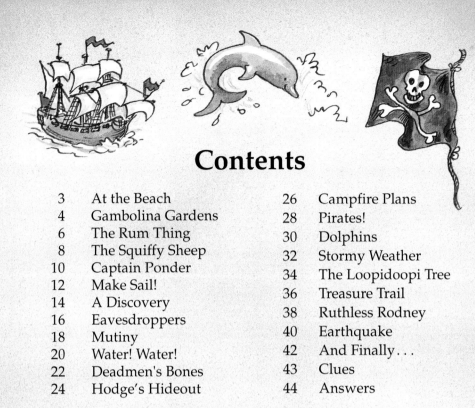

Contents

About this book

Mutiny at Crossbones Bay is an action adventure on the high seas, packed with pirates, treasure and mutineers. Throughout the book there are lots of tricky puzzles which you must solve in order to understand the next part of the story. If you get stuck there are clues on page 43 and you can check the answers on pages 44 to 48.

At the Beach

Tom and Mandy were staying with their Uncle Derek on Gambolina, the largest of the Wayward Islands. Their uncle was a scientist and always busy at his laboratory. Today, as usual, Tom and Mandy were at the beach.

Mandy had just finished reading her fifth book on pirates that week.

"Phew! I'm getting too hot sitting here," she said. "Let's go somewhere cooler."

Tom pointed to an article in the local paper. "There's a grand sale in the botanical gardens," he said. "It might be worth looking at."

"Great," said Mandy. "Let's go."

Botanical Research Foundation in urgent need of funds

from our scientific and garage sales correspondent

Professor Devver

Professor Ernest N. Devver, head of Gambolina's Botanical Research Foundation says that the foundation is in danger of closing 'in a matter of weeks' unless new funds can be found.

The foundation, set up to study the medicinal properties of the flora of the Wayward Islands, also owns the Gambolina Botanical Gardens.

So far, the Botanical Research Foundation has created many valuable medicines, including *Noburp*, the popular indigestion remedy.

A "grand sale" is planned for 2.30 this Saturday, in a last ditch ...nt to stop the door closing on the foundation and the gar... ...y last time.

Gambolina Gardens

The botanical gardens were bustling with people. There were plenty of stalls with every kind of junk.

"Wow!" said Mandy, looking around in amazement. "They're selling just about everything."

"Look", said Tom. "There's the man whose picture was in the paper."

The professor's stall was piled high with interesting objects. Some of them could have come straight out of the pirate books Mandy had been reading.

"Look at this," she said, grabbing what looked like a pirate hat.

Then Mandy saw something strange. Before she could investigate, the ground began to tremble and shudder.

"Help!" Tom cried, as he and Mandy lost their footing and the things on the stall began to tumble around them.

What had Mandy seen?

The Rum Thing

T he next moment, the ground seemed to open beneath them and they were falling . . . falling . . . falling . . .

Frantically they clung to one another. What was happening?

Then suddenly they were lying, bruised and dazed, on a hard floor. Mandy was about to cry out but Tom put his hand over her mouth and stopped her. What was going on?

Small wonder that Davy Jones wants a pirate's life.

I've heard said two youngsters jumped ship to avoid all that washing and watering.

Anything sounds better than life under Captain Ponder aboard the *Squiffy Sheep.*

They found themselves in a candlelit room full of people in old-fashioned clothes. The gardens had disappeared.

From their dark corner, Tom and Mandy listened to the conversation, desperately trying to make sense of things.

Then a door opened, throwing light onto Tom and Mandy.

"Eek!" screamed a woman, dropping a tray of food.

"And who are you?" shouted the landlord.

Everything was happening so quickly, Tom and Mandy didn't know what to say.

"They must be those two that jumped off the *Squiffy Sheep* that Davy Jones was telling us all about," said a man smoking a long clay pipe.

"Then they must go straight back there!" said the landlord. "I won't have it said that I've sheltered deserters. Only honest seafolk drink at *The Rum Thing Tavern*."

"Of course they do, landlord," said a man with a pigtail. "Of course they do. I'll take them back to the ship myself. I have an errand that way, as it happens."

"But . . . But . . ." cried Mandy.

"No buts!" said the man. He grabbed Mandy and Tom in a vice-like grip, then marched them roughly out into the street.

As they passed through the door, Tom glanced at a poster and made a rather startling discovery.

What has Tom realized?

The Squiffy Sheep

If the poster on the wall of the tavern was genuine, they must have gone back in time.

Not only that, but they were now in the clutches of a wanted man and suspected of being deserters!

Before they had a chance to get away, they were pushed into a boat and rowed out to a ship in the bay.

"Ahoy there, Davy Jones," the man called, as they drew near.

"What is it?" said Jones, looking over the side.

"Those two young deserters you told us about. They're here. And I've a letter for you."

"Deserters? What des . . ? Oh, yes! Of course – the tavern," replied Davy Jones. "Err . . . Send them up on deck. And quickly!"

"Give him this," said the man, handing Tom a letter. "Tell him to get it read, then to destroy it. Now climb aboard."

Tom and Mandy scrambled up the side of the ship. As soon as they were on deck, Davy Jones snatched the letter from Tom and hid it in his pocket. He seemed rather flustered.

"We're not deserters!" cried Tom loudly.

"Quiet!" hissed Davy Jones. "Yikes, here's the Master!"

They turned around, but to Tom and Mandy's surprise, an old woman stood behind them.

At least you young'uns look well scrubbed. Under the fingernails too, I hope?

"Who's this that you have with you, Mister Jones?" she demanded. "You know I don't allow visitors on board. They usually bring dirt with them."

"Err . . . volunteers, Ma'am," mumbled Davy Jones.

"What luck!" said the old woman. She turned to Mandy and Tom. "There are few rules aboard the *Squiffy Sheep* except keep clean, eat healthy and keep the plants watered. We leave at first light, Mister Jones. I'll take these two to meet the Captain."

Captain Ponder

The Master led Tom and Mandy along the deck to the Captain's cabin. They went inside.

"What is it, Grandma?" a voice called out from among dozens of plants in pots. A man stood before them, peering through an elegant magnifying glass.

Mandy thought back to *The Rum Thing Tavern*. From the way people had been talking there, she had expected Captain Ponder to be an evil tyrant.

"New recruits, grandson," said the old woman. "And they've sailed before, I can tell."

"But that was in the twentieth century . . . I mean *will be* in the twentieth century," Mandy blurted out. "We've come back in time . . ."

"Stuff and nonsense," said the Master. "Now I must go and supervise the crew's wash hour. Hurry up and plot our course on that chart. There'll be light duties for you both if you can do it. We're heading for Bandicoon Island."

Tom and Mandy studied the chart, trying desperately to remember their sailing lessons, but where should they start?

What course should they plot?

— Master's Log —

Thurs. Left Dimmwitt Island and headed for Rosebun Island. Made good progress.

Fri. Captain changes his mind (after we've travelled 120 miles. Sometimes I despair of my grandson) and we set a new course N.E. The crew seem rather fed up. Double ration of lemons before bed.

Sat. Sight island at 6 bells of the forenoon (just as we're having elevenses). Drop anchor in the bay on the north side. Quite a town has sprung up since my last (unhappy) visit here. Some of the crew go ashore to the tavern. I must make sure they're not late back as we leave first thing in the morning.

GOVERNMENT FLAG SIGNALS

LOOKING FOR — ABOUT TO
POTATOES — SURRENDER
ALL — ATTACK
WE ARE — HAVE TEA
A LOAD OF — UNDER
SEA SICK — PARROT
PIRATES — A FIG...
AT SEA — HE...

number of plants
...e) have to be
...d and watered
we shall get
...t of the
...Island.
...must
...h.

Bandicoon Island
Numskull Island
Screwloose Island
Traphic Islands
Semolina Island
Rosebun Island
Dimmwitt Island
Mandolina Island

~ Miles ~
10 20 30 40 50

N
W   E
S

Make Sail!

Now Tom and Mandy knew that they'd not only gone back in time, but to a different place too.

The next morning, the *Squiffy Sheep* set sail. Mandy and Tom tackled their tasks for the day. And hard work they were too. So much for light duties!

> Mister Jones? Order the men to start watering the plants immediately.

> And don't get them dirty.

They had to hold the steering wheel for hours and hours, keeping the ship on the right course.

They had to polish the cannons and scrub the decks until everything was perfectly clean.

They had to mend the ropes and patch the sails, making sure that everything was ship-shape.

And it didn't end there . . . The Master then sent them to help Cook in the galley.

Cook was sick. He was lying ill in his hammock, groaning and clutching his stomach.

SUPPER

ONION STEW,
SALT BEEF
or EGG SALAD.
served with:
POTATOES,
PORRIDGE
or SHIP'S BISCUITS.
followed by:
COFFEE.
TEA or GROG.

Galley Rules

1. The Captain and the Master (Grandma) always have different food and drink.
2. The crew never eat or drink the same as either the Captain or Grandma.
3. The Captain doesn't like grog or porridge but loves onion stew.
4. The Master won't eat salt beef (which is always served with potatoes).
5. Coffee is only served with healthy egg salad.

It was clear that Mandy and Tom were going to have to decide what everyone should eat. Cook wasn't much help. All he told them was that the Captain, the Master and the crew must all have different food.

"And you'd better get it right," he warned. "Last time I gave the Master the wrong food, I was in big trouble and had to spend all night at the top of the mast."

Who is served which food?

A Discovery

Tom and Mandy had to go to the top of the mast after all. Captain Ponder wanted his socks dried. Davy Jones had managed to soak them when he was on plant-watering duty.

"They'll dry quickly up there," said the Master. "And the bracing wind will do you both the power of good."

They clung tightly to the ropes as they climbed all the way to the crow's nest.

They looked down at a group of sailors huddled together on the deck. It was easy to pick out Davy Jones's figure among them. When the Master appeared they all went back to work rather quickly.

"They were probably worried that she was going to tell them all to have a bath in lemon juice!" Tom laughed.

"Or to water some more of her grandson's plants," Mandy grinned, thinking of the Captain.

Don't let the new recruits find out . . .

That afternoon, Mandy was sent to collect eggs from the hen coop. This time, she spotted two sailors huddled together. They were whispering about a secret meeting to be held after supper.

Mandy tried to listen and look busy at the same time. She reached into the coop for another egg in the straw. Instead, she pulled out a sheet of crumpled paper. There was a coded message on it.

As soon as she could, Mandy slipped away to find Tom. She smoothed out the paper and showed him the message.

Tom stared at the mass of meaningless words. "This is the letter I gave to Davy Jones," he said. "But it doesn't make any sense." Together, they tried to decipher it.

What is the secret message?

DLCN TEA AIGHE GEEPE THFE
IEA SHE SNWIE ENMRI SOGOB
STNAET AGIV AD AETRM MORO
AHN NNMRE LEGS LMHA OULTL
BEOD MERDL TRIR BETT CDHD

Eavesdroppers

"Pirates? Signals? Disable the cannons?" puzzled Tom. "There's something very dangerous going on here."

"Yes," agreed Mandy with excitement. "Why don't we listen in on the meeting tonight and find out what's being planned?"

"Good idea," said Tom. "But we'll need to get there early and find a good hiding place."

After supper, they stuffed their hammocks to look as if they were asleep in them. Then, they crept along to the lower deck. There was an empty barrel which seemed an ideal hiding place. They didn't have to wait long.

Just as things were beginning to get interesting, Tom sneezed. Seconds later their hiding place was discovered.

"You're crazy to trust pirates," Mandy blurted out as they sprawled onto the deck.

"It's spies like you we don't trust," snarled Davy Jones. "Lock 'em up, men!"

Protesting loudly, the two eavesdroppers were dragged to the Powder Room. They were thrown inside and the door locked behind them.

"Now we're sunk," said Mandy. "We'll never get out of here."

"We might be able to escape," said Tom, examining the lock.

"Be careful!" warned Mandy. "This is gunpowder. One spark and we'll be blown into next week."

In which order should Tom slide back the bolts to safely unlock the door?

Mutiny

Free at last, Mandy and Tom arrived on deck. The dark mass of an island loomed on the starboard bow.

The deck was deserted. They ran straight to the nearest doorway and burst through it.

To their horror, they found themselves in a cabin with Davy Jones and his mutineers. The Captain and the Master were tied up in the middle of the room.

"Perhaps our two young spies should join them," said Davy Jones. "Throw them all in the boat and row them ashore!"

Sailors grabbed Tom and Mandy, and roughly bundled them down the ship's side into the rowing boat. There, their hands were tied tightly behind their backs.

When they reached the beach of Crossbones Bay, the mutineers dumped them on the sand.

"Listen, me hearties. Let's hoist the Jolly Roger and go in search of pirates and adventure," said Davy Jones excitedly. "I'm your captain now."

"No more washing and watering!" cried the mutineers.

"Ruffians! Mutineers! You'll be in deep water for this!" the Master yelled after them.

When the mutineers got back to the *Squiffy Sheep,* they started throwing things overboard.

From the shore, Captain Ponder could see lemons and plants bobbing about in the sea

"Oh, no! NO!" he wailed in a pitiful voice. "My beautiful plants! My children!"

As the sun rose it began to get hot on the beach.

"It could be worse," said Tom. "At least they've left us a full bottle of water."

"But they could have untied our hands," Mandy protested.

What was going to happen to them now they were marooned at Crossbones Bay? If only they could get free of the ropes. Then, noticing the things that had fallen from the Captain's pocket, Mandy had an idea.

How can they get free?

Water! Water!

The moment that the Master's hands were untied, she got up and started running up the beach cursing the mutineers.

"Idiots! You can't even sail!" she cried. The *Squiffy Sheep* was sailing in a circle. The sailors had forgotten to raise the anchor.

"Arggghhh! Wait till I get my hands on you!" screamed the Master, jumping up and down. "My lovely clean ship."

If there hadn't been several sharks circling in the bay she probably would have leaped into the sea, swum out to the ship and recaptured it single-handed.

Instead, the Master beat her fists with frustration on the trunk of a palm tree.Unfortunately for her, this dislodged a coconut which fell and knocked her out.

"Oh no . . . Grandma!" wailed the Captain, going frantic. "Where's the water bottle?" he cried, grabbing it from Tom. The Captain uncorked it and splashed water over his grandma's face.

"Hey!" shouted Mandy. "That's all we've got!" But it was too late. The Captain had emptied the whole bottle.

"Now we'll have to go looking for more water," said Tom.

As they set off along the beach they watched the *Squiffy Sheep* sail out of the bay. The mutineers had managed to raise the anchor.

"Now we're well and truly stuck here," said Mandy. "Look, there seems to be a path!"

They followed the path for a while and came to a spot where it divided into three.

If it is water that you seek, listen to the words we've been taught to speak.

And no running downhill in between. *Squawk. Squawk.*

Squawk. As far as I can see, all the water should be left alone.

Squawk. Your right and wrong are both the same. *Squawk.*

"Now which way?" said Mandy. "I hope we find some water soon. I'm getting thirsty."

Suddenly there was a series of squawks. Looking up, Tom and Mandy saw three parrots perching on a branch nearby.

All three birds started talking at once. It was Mandy and Tom who were speechless.

"They're telling us which path leads to the water!" said Mandy.

Which path should they take?

Deadmen's Bones

Tom and Mandy set off up the path, wondering who had taught the parrots to speak.

The farther they went, the steeper the path became. The undergrowth was less tangled and the trees began to thin out. Scrambling over some boulders, they found themselves in a grassy clearing with a wonderful view of the island.

"Look, there's the *Squiffy Sheep*," said Mandy. "She hasn't moved very far. She's only in the next bay."

"I don't think the new Captain Jones and his crew can be very good sailors," Tom grinned.

They turned to continue on their way and Tom stopped to look at an odd-shaped boulder. It was set apart from the rest.

"It's got letters carved on it," said Tom excitedly.

"It must be a gravestone!" said Mandy. "Perhaps it belongs to the person who taught the parrots to speak in riddles."

They cleared away the moss that covered the stone and read the inscription.

"I've read about that ship in one of my books," said Mandy. "She was captained by a pirate called One-Eyed Hodge. He had an enormous hoard of priceless pirate treasure which has never been found."

"Maybe Gudgeon is buried with the treasure, if he's buried here at all," said Tom. Then he realized that he could see a hidden message.

What does it say?

Hodge's Hideout

Tom and Mandy carried on up the path. Before long, the thunderous sound of falling water reached their ears. They turned a corner and there, in front of them, was a magnificent waterfall. It dropped hundreds of feet into a large pool of clear water.

They would be able to fill the water bottle, then look for the secret hideout mentioned in the carved message.

"My feet hurt," said Tom. He sat down on a large flat rock beside the waterfall to take his shoes off. Mandy joined him.

Suddenly the stone tipped forward, and they started sliding off the edge. "Help!" they yelled, frantically trying to hold on, but the stone was so smooth they just kept on sliding, faster and faster . . . straight into the heart of the waterfall.

Seconds later they were spluttering on a bed of old coconut husks.

"We're behind the waterfall!" cried Mandy in amazement. "We've found the hideout!"

"I don't see any treasure," said Mandy, as they peered about.

But Tom wasn't listening. He had found a crumbling piece of parchment.

"It's not a treasure map," said Mandy, as they pieced it together. She tried to read the writing.

"Not a map, maybe," said Tom, "But they could be clues leading to the treasure. I wish we had some tape to stick it back together."

"It hasn't been invented yet, silly," grinned Mandy.

Can you fit the pieces together and read the writing?

Campfire Plans

They couldn't make sense of the list of clues at all.

"It obviously has to do with the treasure, but it's all muddled up," said Mandy with a frown.

"We'll have to sort it out later," said Tom. "We really ought to get back."

Clinging to the rock face, they edged their way along past the torrent of water.

Back in the bright sunshine, Tom filled the bottle up with water from the pool.

They set off down the track. Their wet clothes soon dried in the hot sun.

Be sure to wash your hands, and gargle with half a bottle of *Dr. Gripe's Remedy.*

By the time they returned to the beach of Crossbones Bay, the sun was beginning to go down. The Captain had got a fire going and was roasting bananas. The Master was recovering from her accident but was a bit confused.

"She thinks I'm Grandpa, her long-lost husband," said the Captain. "And she insists you call her Grandma."

Tom and Mandy handed Captain Ponder the water bottle.

"Thank you," he said. "You know, I can't understand why my crew mutinied. "I was very fair."

"It was Davy Jones's idea," Mandy explained. "He and your crew didn't like having to water your plants and wash in lemon juice all the time."

They told the Captain everything they had seen and heard since falling back in time.

"So Davy Jones is planning to join up with some pirates," said the Captain." I can't see why any self-respecting pirates should want him in their crew."

"Perhaps it's the *Squiffy Sheep* the pirates really want . . . and they're tricking Davy Jones into handing her over to them," Mandy suggested.

"I can't see that it makes any difference," said the Captain. "Either way we're stuck here."

"Maybe we could retake the *Squiffy Sheep* at dawn?" said Mandy. "She's in the next bay."

"There's no wind so she can't sail anywhere," Tom added with growing excitement. "And Jones and the crew are bound to be asleep if we sneak up on them."

"But how would we get out to the ship?" said the Captain. "We can't swim, not with all those sharks in the water. Even if we could, I'm not leaving Grandma behind. We need to build a boat."

"I think I know where we can find one," said Tom.

Where has Tom remembered seeing a boat?

Pirates

Luckily the old boat didn't leak. Just before dawn, they all clambered in to it, and rowed out to the *Squiffy Sheep*.

"Are we going fishing?" asked Grandma (as Mandy and Tom now called the Master). She was still feeling a bit dazed.

The mutineers were all snoring loudly when Tom and Mandy crept on board. They gathered up the weapons and helped Grandma and the Captain on deck.

The Captain fired a pistol into the air to wake up the mutineers. They didn't know what was happening. Then Mandy saw something that made her blood run cold.

"Sail on the port bow!" she yelled. "It's PIRATES! Raise the anchor! Make sail!"

"But that's the *Battered Cod*," said Davy Jones, looking at the ship on the horizon. "That's Ruthless Rodney's ship. I planned the whole mutiny with him. He's friendly."

"No he's not!" shouted Mandy. "Look. He's hoisted the red pennant. That means a fight!"

"Why, the double-crossing swine," cried Jones. His shouts were interrupted by a puff of smoke and a loud BOOM from the *Battered Cod*. A cannon ball fell just short of the *Squiffy Sheep*.

"Now do you believe us?" said Tom. "We must try and escape!"

Tom grabbed the chart. If only they could cross the shallow lagoon but the *Squiffy Sheep* needed three fathoms of water or more if she wasn't to get stuck. There had to be a way.

Can you find a way across the shallow lagoon?

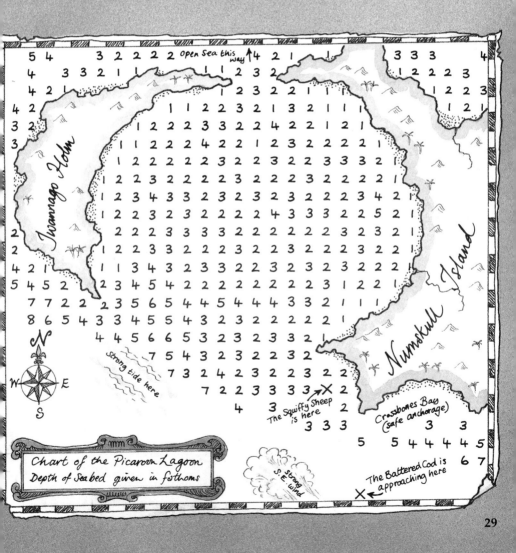

Chart of the Picaroon Lagoon
Depth of Seabed given in fathoms

Dolphins

As the *Squiffy Sheep* sailed through the gap and made for the open sea, the *Battered Cod* appeared beside them. She was getting closer every minute. Tom and Mandy could see the pirates gathered on her deck and they were worryingly close.

"Oh dear," cried Captain Ponder. "We're not going to make it. We can't use more sails because the wind's too strong. We're going to have to . . . er . . . fight!"

"Stand by to repel all boarders!" Mandy shouted.

Everybody began to panic. They hadn't the faintest idea what to do. They'd never been in a fight before.

"Oh, help . . . HELP!" wailed Davy Jones.

But suddenly the *Battered Cod* dropped behind.

"Her mast has snapped!" yelled Tom excitedly. "The wind must have been too strong for her." Everybody cheered. At last they had escaped the pirates.

"Hey!" shouted Mandy, "Look. Dolphins!" There were five of them dashing through the water around the ship.

"Huh?" said Davy Jones. "They're like the one on my arm." He rolled up his sleeve to reveal a tattoo. "It was copied from the one my grandfather had."

"Follow the Dolphin's lead!" shouted Mandy, suddenly. "That's what it says on the parchment. This must be the key to the clues. We only have to work this out and we'll know where to start looking for the treasure!"

Which clues should they follow?

Stormy Weather

Suddenly, the weather grew worse and the wind grew even stronger. Dark clouds appeared on the horizon.

High above the deck, the sailors battled with the wind to take down the sails before they were ripped to ribbons.

Great waves pounded the sides of the ship as, together, Tom and Mandy struggled to keep hold of the helm

A huge wave broke over the rail and crashed, foaming and frothing, onto the deck. Tom and Mandy clung desperately to the ropes as they were very nearly swept overboard.

"Hold on!" cried Davy Jones coming to their rescue. Bravely plunging through the swirling water, he pulled them toward the stern of the *Squiffy Sheep* and helped them to safety.

The storm was slowly dying away when, suddenly through the surf, Mandy spied yet another danger.

"Rocks!" she screamed. "Let go the anchor!" She frantically spun the wheel, trying to turn the ship away.

The anchor splashed into the water. The *Squiffy Sheep* was safe at last. Now they could go and get some rest.

On deck next morning, Tom and Mandy found the Captain staring hopelessly at the charts. "I've no idea where we are," he said. "I'm afraid navigating's not my thing."

"Mandy, we're back at Gambolina!" said Tom in amazement. "That's Gungho Mountain, remember? The guidebook said it's 2,700 feet high."

"We'll need to pinpoint our position," said Mandy. "The rocks here are treacherous and there's only one safe route into the bay."

They took a reading with the quadrant and compass. Now they could plot the course.

What is the ship's current position on the map?

The Loopidoopi Tree

A s they dropped anchor in Gambolina Bay, Mandy realized that they were right at the start of the treasure trail.

"Of course," said Tom. "This is the Bay of the Hammer Rock. Look over there." The curiously shaped outcrop towered above them.

"So this is where the Botanical Gardens will be in two centuries time," said Mandy. It was odd to see the bay with no buildings or people sunbathing.

Only Grandma stayed on board the *Squiffy Sheep*. She wanted to clean it from bilge to poop.

Captain Ponder wasn't all that interested in treasure but he went along to look for unusual plants.

From the beach they went to the base of the Hammer Rock and then headed northwest to the great tree.

Suddenly the Captain gave a whoop of delight. "It's a Loopidoopi Tree!" he cried.

While the Captain climbed the tree, everybody else was puzzling over the next clue of the treasure trail. They were gathered around an old sundial carved into a rock.

"This must point to the *Cave of Nightmares*," said Tom, remembering the list of clues.

Where is the cave?

Treasure Trail

Tom, Mandy and the crew of the *Squiffy Sheep* left Captain Ponder sitting beneath the Loopidoopi tree and made their way to the cave. They studied the parchment, picked up their ship's lanterns, then went inside.

The cave went down steeply, the tunnel twisting and turning. Mandy screamed.

They were faced by a skeleton holding a sign. Beyond it, the path divided into three. Each of these paths was a bridge, supported on pillars over one hundred feet high.

One wrong step would mean certain disaster.

Which route leads to One-Eyed Hodge's pirate hoard?

HENCEFORTH,
CHOOSE YOUR PATH WITH CARE,
AND BE, WITH CAUTION, BOLD.
NOT ALL THE TREASURE'S REALLY THERE,
NOR ALL THAT GLITTERS, GOLD!

Ruthless Rodney

Once they had successfully reached the treasure, Tom, Mandy and the crew made their way back across the perilous path. The chest was so full of gold, silver and jewels that they could only just lift it.

Blinking in the sunlight, they found Captain Ponder sitting beneath the Loopidoopi tree where they had left him. Even he seemed pleased to see their haul.

"I'll be able to finance more expeditions now," he cried. "And build an institute for studying the plants of these islands."

They all set off back to the beach. "We're rich! We're rich!" sang Davy Jones.

"Oh no you're not!" yelled a voice like thunder. "Surround them, lads, and relieve them of their burden."

"Ruthless Rodney!" gasped Davy Jones. "To think I wanted to join you."

"Hah, yah lily-livered landlubber, Jones! I might have known that you'd flee rather than stay and fight like a pirate, " laughed Ruthless Rodney. "And now I have your ship too."

"Do you mean *my* ship?" stammered Captain Ponder.

"If you're the captain of the *Squiffy Sheep*, then yes! Fancy leaving her without a watch on board." The pirate looked very pleased with himself. "With the wind up again and our mast repaired, I thought we should pay you a visit . . ."

Rodney grinned, showing a fine set of black teeth, and the pirates laughed toothless laughs.

But Mandy wasn't at all sure that they would get away with it as easily as they thought. She'd seen a couple of things that made her think differently.

What has Mandy seen?

Earthquake

"Not so fast, Rodney Reckitt!" cried a voice that made even Ruthless Rodney stand stock still. His mouth dropped wide open. It was Grandma.

Now listen, my long-lost husband, that ship that has just dropped anchor is the pirate-hunter *Grabbum*. I'm on good terms with the captain's wife, so you'd better do as I say . . .

"Ruth, my sweet . . ." he mumbled under his breath. He dropped his pistols and sank to his knees. "It's been so long . . ." Ruthless Rodney gulped. "I am Ruth-less no longer."

The pirates had all huddled in a small group. They were trembling. Captain Rodney had met his match, and they didn't know what to do.

Suddenly the earth began to shake and shudder beneath them. "An earthquake?" yelled Davy Jones in terror. Everybody began to panic.

Pirates and sailors rushed in different directions, scrambling every which way as the ground cracked beneath their feet.

The treasure was dropped in the confusion, landing in a hole that had opened up in the earth. Then Captain Ponder slipped and the Loopidoopi seed pod fell out of his hands and into the hole as well!

"Oh no . . ." he wailed. He'd found his Grandpa and lost the Loopidoopi pod in one afternoon!

The ground began to shake even more violently and Tom and Mandy lost their footing. Then they were falling and the earth seemed to close over them. All was darkness.

"Help!" cried Mandy.

"All right, all right, wait a moment," said a voice. It was Professor Devver. He helped them out from under the collapsed stall.

"We had an earth tremor," said the professor. "Nothing serious."

They could hardly believe it – they were back in the Botanical Gardens and in their own time! Suddenly Tom saw something that gave him an idea.

"Things might turn out even better than you'd hoped," he said.

What has Tom seen?

And Finally...

Pirate treasure found in Botanical Gardens!

Botanical Research Foundation saved by children's discovery

from our financial and racketeering correspondent

Following last Saturday's earth tremor on Gambolina, two children found a priceless hoard of 18th century pirate treasure in the Botanical Gardens. The money raised from the sale of the treasure will go toward funding the Research Foundation well into the middle of the next century. The children, Tom and Mandy Mustard told amazed reporters that they had noticed that ̶ ̶ ̶ ̶ ̶ ̶ ̶ ̶ing glinting under

Tom and Mandy Mustard, whose find has saved the Botanical Research Foundation

Botanical Research Foundation to be renamed "Ponder Institute"

from our renaming of foundations correspondent

Rare tree identified at last

from our rare tree identification correspondent

Scientists have at last correctly identified the largest tree in Gambolina Botanical Gardens, long known as the Wigwam Tree, or *Perplexitas Vulgaris*. It is in fact a Loopidoopi Tree, or *Perspicacia Longifolium Ponderii*, until now thought to be extinct. The last specimen w̶ ̶ ̶ been recorded by Captain ̶ ̶ ̶ Ponder in 1743. It was Capt̶

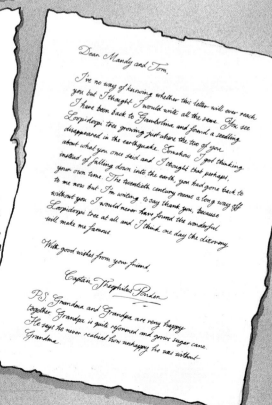

Dear Mandy and Tom,

I've no way of knowing whether this letter will ever reach you but I thought I would write all the same. You see I have been back to Gambolina and found a seedling Loopidoopi tree growing just where the two of you disappeared in the earthquake. Somehow I got thinking about what you once said and I thought that perhaps, instead of falling down into the earth, you had gone back to your own time. The twentieth century seems a long way off to me now but I'm writing to say thank you, because without you I would never have found the wonderful Loopidoopi tree at all and I think one day the discovery will make me famous.

With good wishes from your friend,

Captain Theophilus Ponder

P.S. Grandma and Grandpa are very happy together. Grandpa is quite reformed and grows sugar cane. He says he never realised how unhappy he was without Grandma.

Clues

Pages 4-5
Look carefully at the things on the stall. Can you see anything that is surprising?

Pages 6-7
Does the description on the poster resemble anyone at the tavern?

Pages 10-11
Start by finding out which island the *Squiffy Sheep* is anchored at.

Pages 12-13
First try to decide what the Master has to eat. Once you've done that it's easy.

Pages 14-15
This isn't really in code at all. Letters don't always have to be read from left to right.

Pages 16-17
Which bolt inside the lock should be pushed across first in order to stop the flint making a spark?

Pages 18-19
Is there anything among the Captain's things that they could use to make a fire to burn the ropes?

Pages 20-21
Each parrot's message could have more than one meaning. Pay attention to what they say.

Pages 22-23
There's an odd mixture of small letters and capitals in this message.

Pages 24-25
Trace the fragments of paper, then fit them together.

Pages 26-27
The boat is within sight of some feathered friends.

Pages 28-29
Remember that the route has to pass through water of three fathoms or more in depth.

Pages 30-31
Look at the numbers in the tattoo. The stars are for the missing numbers in a sequence. Could they be the key to the parchment that Mandy and Tom found in Hodge's hideout?

Pages 32-33
All of the information that you need is here on this page.

Pages 34-35
The shadow on the sundial points to the cave but what time of day is 'six bells of the forenoon'? Look back to page 11 to find out.

Pages 36-37
A clue on the parchment will give you a start but you'll still have to tread very carefully and not lose your balance!

Pages 38-39
What do the flags on the ship mean? Look on page 11 to find out. And can you see somebody familiar hiding nearby?

Pages 40-41
That large tree looks familiar. How did it get there? And didn't the treasure end up in the same place as the seed pod this tree must have grown from?

Answers

Pages 4-5

Mandy has seen a letter on the stall circled here. It is addressed to Mandy and Tom!

Pages 6-7

Tom has realized that the man who is marching them out of *The Rum Thing Tavern* fits the description of the man in the wanted poster. He has a scar on his right cheek and only half of his left thumb. And the poster is dated 1743!

Pages 10-11

Mandy and Tom look at the Master's log and plot the course that the *Squiffy Sheep* has already taken.

They went west to Rosebun Island for 120 miles and then changed direction, heading northeast. The island which they dropped anchor at must therefore be Semolina. Their route is marked here.

To reach Bandicoon Island, they must, therefore, plot a northwesterly course.

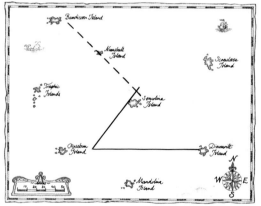

Pages 12-13

The Master has egg salad served with porridge and followed by coffee.
The Captain has onion stew with ship's biscuits and tea.
The crew has salt beef with potatoes, followed by grog.

Pages 14-15

This is not in code at all. The letters are simply written from top to bottom, instead of across the page. The message reads:

DISABLE THE CANNONS AND THEN
MEET ME AS ARRANGED
I WILL GIVE THE AGREED SIGNAL
REMEMBER THE PIRATES' MOTTO:
MUCH GOLD FOR THE BOLD

Pages 16-17

Tom and Mandy can safely unlock the door by sliding the top bolt before the bottom one. If the bottom bolt is slid across first, the flint lever is released and, flicking across, makes a spark. If the top bolt is slid across first, it holds the flint in place, so that the bottom bolt can then be slid across without any danger.

Pages 18-19

Mandy sees a magnifying glass among the Captain's belongings. They can use this to focus the sun's rays on the ropes and burn through them.

Pages 20-21

The parrots' words have double meanings. The 'right' which is wrong in the message "right and wrong are both the same" refers to the right-hand path.

"No running downhill in between" isn't an instruction to walk, but means that there is no water at the end of the middle path.

". . . the water should be left alone" means that it can only be found down the left-hand path. It is this path that Tom and Mandy should take.

Pages 22-23

When the small letters on the gravestone are put together and broken down into words, they say:

CLOSE TO THE
WATERFALL IS A
SECRET HIDEOUT

Pages 24-25

The pieces of parchment fit together as shown here. It makes a list of clues which might prove to be useful later!

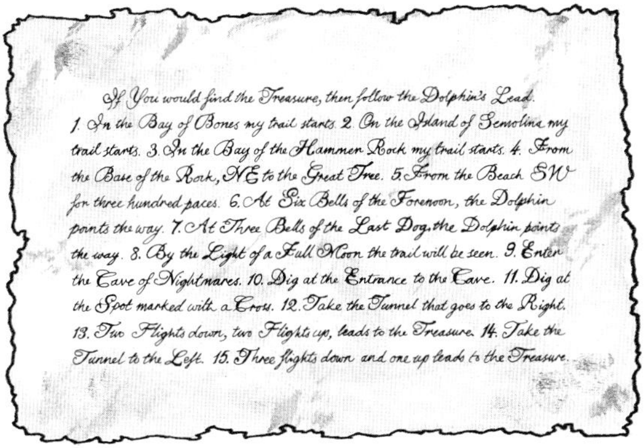

If You would find the Treasure, then follow the Dolphin's Lead. 1. In the Bay of Bones my trail starts. 2. On the Island of Semolina my trail starts. 3. In the Bay of the Hammer Rock my trail starts. 4. From the Base of the Rock, NE to the Great Tree. 5. From the Beach SW for three hundred paces. 6. At Six Bells of the Forenoon, the Dolphin points the way. 7. At Three Bells of the Last Dog, the Dolphin points the way. 8. By the Light of a Full Moon the trail will be seen. 9. Enter the Cave of Nightmares. 10. Dig at the Entrance to the Cave. 11. Dig at the Spot marked with a Cross. 12. Take the Tunnel that goes to the Right. 13. Two Flights down, two Flights up, leads to the Treasure. 14. Take the Tunnel to the Left. 15. Three flights down and one up leads to the Treasure.

Pages 26-27

Tom remembers having seen an old boat somewhere on the island. He hopes that it isn't full of holes, so they will be able to use it.

The boat is near the tree that the parrots are perched in on page 21.

Pages 28-29

The course that the *Squiffy Sheep* needs to take to reach the open sea and safety is marked here in red.

It is the only safe route for a ship needing a depth of three fathoms of water or more.

Chart of the Picaroon Lagoon. Depth of Seabed given in fathoms.

Pages 30-31

The numbers in Davy Jones's tattoo are in a special order with the missing numbers marked with stars. The second number is the first +1, the third number is the second +2 and so on, the difference between the numbers increasing by one every time.

The full sequence of numbers is therefore: 3, 4, 6, 9, 13

This tells them which of the clues on the parchment will lead them to the treasure. The others are just red herrings.

Pages 32-33

From the table, a 'Vertical Quadrant Angle' of ten degrees combined with a height of 2,700 feet (Gungho Mountain) gives a distance of two and a half miles.

Tom and Mandy know that Gungho Mountain is northeast of them, so the *Squiffy Sheep* is here.

Pages 34-35

Clue 6 on the parchment says that "at six bells of the forenoon, the dolphin points the way".

The "dolphin" is the sundial. It gives the time by casting a shadow on the numbers around the base. "Six bells of the forenoon" is eleven o'clock. Tom and Mandy know this because the Master's log on page 11 mentions that six bells of the forenoon is elevenses time – eleven o'clock in the morning. XI is the Roman number eleven. So, when the shadow falls on this number of the sundial, it will point in the direction of the Cave of Nightmares.

Pages 36-37

Clue 13 on the parchment says that "two flights down, two flights up, leads to the treasure".

The route to the real treasure is marked here in red.

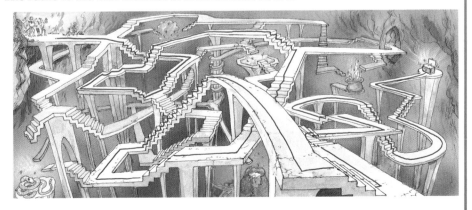

Pages 38-39

Mandy has seen another ship in the bay besides the *Squiffy Sheep* and it is flying flag signals. From the book on page 11 shown here, Mandy knows that these mean: WE ARE LOOKING FOR PIRATES.

Mandy has also seen Grandma hiding here behind the rock.

Pages 40-41

Tom has seen a huge tree behind the collapsed stall and recognizes it as a Loopidoopi tree. It must have grown from the seed swallowed by the earthquake back in the eighteenth century.

Tom wonders what happened to the treasure that tumbled in the hole before the seed. Then he spots something glinting in the crack that has just opened by the tree's roots.

This edition first published in 2006 by Usborne Publishing Ltd., 83-85 Saffron Hill, London, EC1N 8RT. www.usborne.com Copyright © 2006, 1994 Usborne Publishing Ltd.